Bugs

by Anne Giulieri

illustrated by Gaston Vanzet

Look down here.

Here comes
a little worm.

The little worm
is down the hole.

The hole is little.

Look up here.

Here comes
a little caterpillar.

The little caterpillar
is on the leaf.

The leaf is little.

Look down here.

Here comes
a little ant.

The little ant
is in the nest.

The nest is big.

Look up here.

Here comes
a little spider.

The little spider is on the web.
The web is big.

capstone®
classroom

Engage Literacy is published by Capstone Classroom,
1710 Roe Crest Drive, North Mankato, Minnesota 56003.
www.capstoneclassroom.com

Originally published in Australia by Hinkler Education,
a division of Hinkler Books Pty Ltd,
Victoria, Australia, 3202.
www.hinklereducation.com.au

Printed in the United States of America in North Mankato, Minnesota
012017   010242R

Bugs
ISBN: 978-1-4296-8934-2

Look!

Here comes a little caterpillar.

1 2 **3** 4 5 6 7 8 9 10 11 12 13 14 15 16 17 18 19 20 21 22 23 24 25

Word Count: 76
RR: 3 GRL: C

ISBN 978-1-4296-8934-2

capstone
classroom

www.capstoneclassroom.com

Here is a Block

by Anne Giulieri

ENGAGE
Literacy

Here is a Block

GRL: C Nonfiction

Word count: 70

Curriculum link: science, creative play

Text type: explanation

High frequency words consolidated:
a, and, down; *goes (academic),* here, is, the

Example inferential questions:
- *Why did the balance scales go down when the girl put the blue block on?*
- *How might the girl make the blue block go up?*

Phonological awareness/graphophonics: initial letter names/sounds; vowel and consonant blends 'ed', 'is'; onset and rime 'r-ed'; word awareness—recognizing words in sentences

Program links:
Here is a Block E-Book
On the Log (F)